Natural Hawai'i

AN INQUISITIVE KID'S GUIDE

Dana Rozier

dot dot books

dotdotbooks.com

dot
dot
books   dotdotbooks.com
Library of Congress Control Number: 2010939938
ISBN: 0-9670750-1-7
ISBN: 978-0-9670750-1-3
Book design by DesignForBooks.com

Acknowledgments

Many thanks to the following people who helped me create this book—Matthew von der Ahe for sharing his knowledge of geology; Kellen Paik for providing his expertise of the Hawaiian language; Michael Rohani, for his extraordinary book design; and my kids, Elizabeth and David McMinn, for their inquisitive spirits.

Contents

Introduction

mahalo for choosing *Natural Hawai'i: An Inquisitive Kid's Guide*. I hope you enjoy reading it as much as I enjoyed creating it!

Some notes about this book

HAWAIIAN LANGUAGE

The Hawaiian alphabet has thirteen characters—seven consonants, five vowels, and a special mark called the 'okina. The 'okina looks like the number six with the round part filled in. The 'okina is a glottal stop. A glottal stop is a brief pause in speaking. A'a is pronounced ah-ah, not aaah.

Another special character in the Hawaiian language is the kahakō which looks like a short line above a vowel. The kahakō means to say that vowel a bit longer than you normally would.

HAWAIIAN NAMES

While most of the plants and animals listed in this book have Hawaiian names, some of the newly introduced species do not. Instead, they are called by their common English name. In some cases, a few of the plants and animals in this book are best known by their common Hawaiian name such as koa, a native Hawaiian tree.

E nanea mai i ka heluhelu 'ana!
Relax and enjoy your reading!

— Dana Rozier

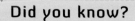

Did you know?

The correct spelling of Hawai'i includes the 'okina. Hawaiian is actually an English word so it is spelled without the 'okina.

USGS Hawaiian Volcano Observatory.

Volcanoes

Quick! If all inhabitants and visitors on Hawai'i decided to jump up and down at one time, how much would the islands sink? A lot? None? How about a teensy-weensy bit?

You're right. The answer is none. While it looks like the Hawaiian Islands are bits of land floating in the sea, they are actually the tops of giant volcanoes rising thousands of feet from the ocean floor.

USGS: Pu`u `O`o Lava fountain.

Hot Spot

How did the Hawaiian volcanoes form under the Pacific Ocean?

Deep in the Earth, below the floor of the Pacific Ocean, a hot spot exists. A hot spot is an area filled with melted rock (magma). Sometimes the magma bursts through Earth's crust. Once the magma is above ground, the liquid is known as lava.

Millions of years ago, lava erupted from the Hawaiian hot spot and flowed onto the ocean floor. As the hot lava encountered the cold water, the lava cooled and hardened. A volcano began to form. The lava from this hot spot continued to erupt for thousands and thousands of years. Each time it erupted, its cooled lava added another layer to the underwater volcano. Eventually, the volcano grew big enough to rise up out of the ocean and the eruptions ultimately stopped. The first Hawaiian Island had been formed! Over millions of years, the chain of Hawaiian Islands was created by this same hot spot.

Did you know?

The hot spot stays in the same place, but the Pacific Plate above it moves. The Pacific Plate is part of the Earth's crust that is underneath the Pacific Ocean. This piece of crust moves very slowly—about at the same rate that your fingernails grow.

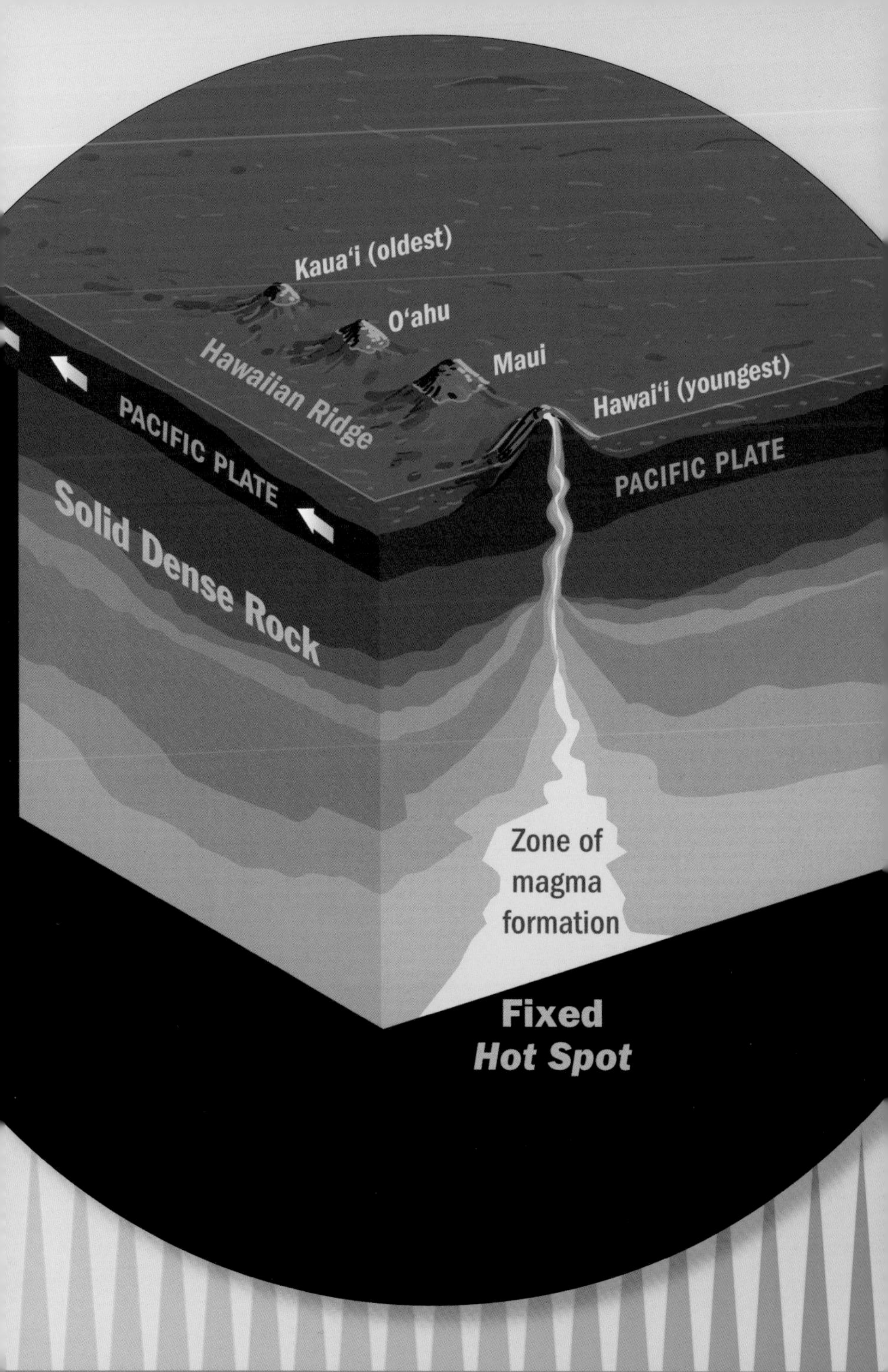

Kaua'i (oldest)

O'ahu

Maui

Hawai'i (youngest)

Hawaiian Ridge

PACIFIC PLATE

PACIFIC PLATE

Solid Dense Rock

Zone of magma formation

Fixed *Hot Spot*

Shield Volcanoes

The volcanoes that make up the Hawaiian Islands are called shield volcanoes. Shield volcanoes have gently sloping slides and can be very large. Some people think the shape of this type of volcano resembles a warrior's shield, so that's how it got its name.

Mauna Loa, a shield volcano on the island of Hawai'i, is the largest volcano on Earth. Since the island is

Hawaiian shield volcano.

still over the hot spot, Mauna Loa continues to erupt and is one of the most active volcanoes in the world. Its last major eruption occurred in 1984. However, another shield volcano on the island of Hawai'i, Kilauea, is erupting today!

Top, Lava flow.

Did you know?

A new underwater volcano is forming off of the southeast coast of Hawai'i. This new volcano, called Lō'ihi (lo·'ee·hee), already rises over three thousand meters (9,482 feet) from the ocean floor. That makes Lō'ihi almost as tall as Mt.Fuji in Japan. Don't plan on a vacation trip to Hawai'i's newest island anytime soon, though. Geologists predict that Lō'ihi won't poke up out of the ocean for at least ten thousand years.

Cinder Cones

Diamond Head and Koko Crater on Oʻahu are examples of another type of volcano found in the Hawaiian Islands—cinder cones. Cinder cones are much smaller than shield volcanoes and are often bowl-shaped. They usually form from eruptions that only last weeks or months, unlike the eruptions from shield volcanoes that can continue for millions of years.

Cinder cones in Haleakalā National Park.

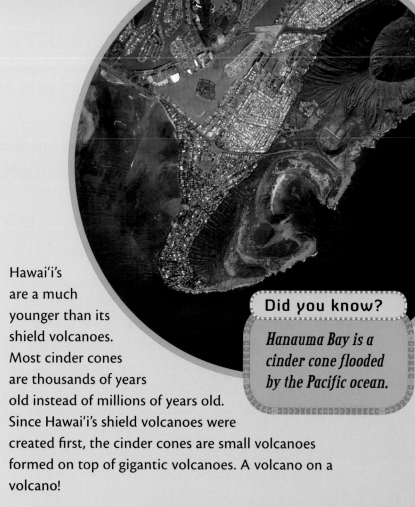

Hawaiʻi's are a much younger than its shield volcanoes. Most cinder cones are thousands of years old instead of millions of years old. Since Hawaiʻi's shield volcanoes were created first, the cinder cones are small volcanoes formed on top of gigantic volcanoes. A volcano on a volcano!

Did you know?

Hanauma Bay is a cinder cone flooded by the Pacific ocean.

Top: Hanauma Bay, Oʻahu, Hawaiʻi. Bottom: Diamond Head, side view.

Erosion

Why aren't most of the Hawaiian Islands shield-shaped anymore? Why does Hawai'i have some green, some red, and some black sand beaches? How did Kaua'i's Waimea Canyon form?

The answer to all these questions is . . . Erosion!

Water and gravity have been wearing down (eroding) the Hawaiian Islands since they formed. Rain and sea water dissolve some of the lava rock and leave other parts of it behind. The crumbs left behind are the sand grains that make up Hawai'i's green, red, black beaches. Lava rock is made up of tiny mineral crystals. Most Hawaiian lava rock is called basalt. The crystals in basalt include olivine and magnetite. Olivine gives green sand beaches their color. Magnetite rusts to add color

Green, red, black sand beach

to red sand beaches. Black sand beaches are ground-up bits of basalt.

Waimea Canyon began forming millions of years ago thanks to a similar process of erosion. First, rain water dissolved lava rock into its separate crystals. As rain carried these crystals towards the sea, the combination of water and crystals acted like sand paper and eroded the lava rock even more. Over eons of time, erosion has worn away enough of Kaua'i's lava rock to form an enormous canyon that is often compared to the Grand Canyon.

Waimea Canyon

Hakalau Forest National Wildlife Refuge

Plants

Imagine the newly formed Hawaiian Islands. The land was nothing more than bare lava rock surrounded by thousands of miles of ocean. Today, the islands are covered with plants. How did the first plant seeds arrive in Hawai'i?

Scientists believe the seeds got carried to the islands by birds, wind, and water. When people started to arrive, they brought different kinds of plants and seeds with them, too.

Today, approximately ninety percent of the plants that you see on Hawai'i are not native to the islands but have been introduced here by humans.

Canoe Plants

Pretend you lived thousands of years ago and were about to set out on a journey by canoe across the ocean to a new homeland. The trip would last at least one month. You would have to take everything you would need in order to survive for the rest of your life.

What would you pack in your canoe?

The Polynesians, the first people to inhabit the Hawaiian Islands, probably asked themselves the same question. In their canoes, they brought pigs, dogs, and chickens for meat. They brought plants that would provide them with food, clothing, shelter, and medicine.

Plants introduced to Hawai'i by the early Polynesians are often referred to as canoe plants.

JAPAN

MICRONESIA

CAROLINE ISLANDS

PAPUA NEW GUINEA

AUSTRALIA

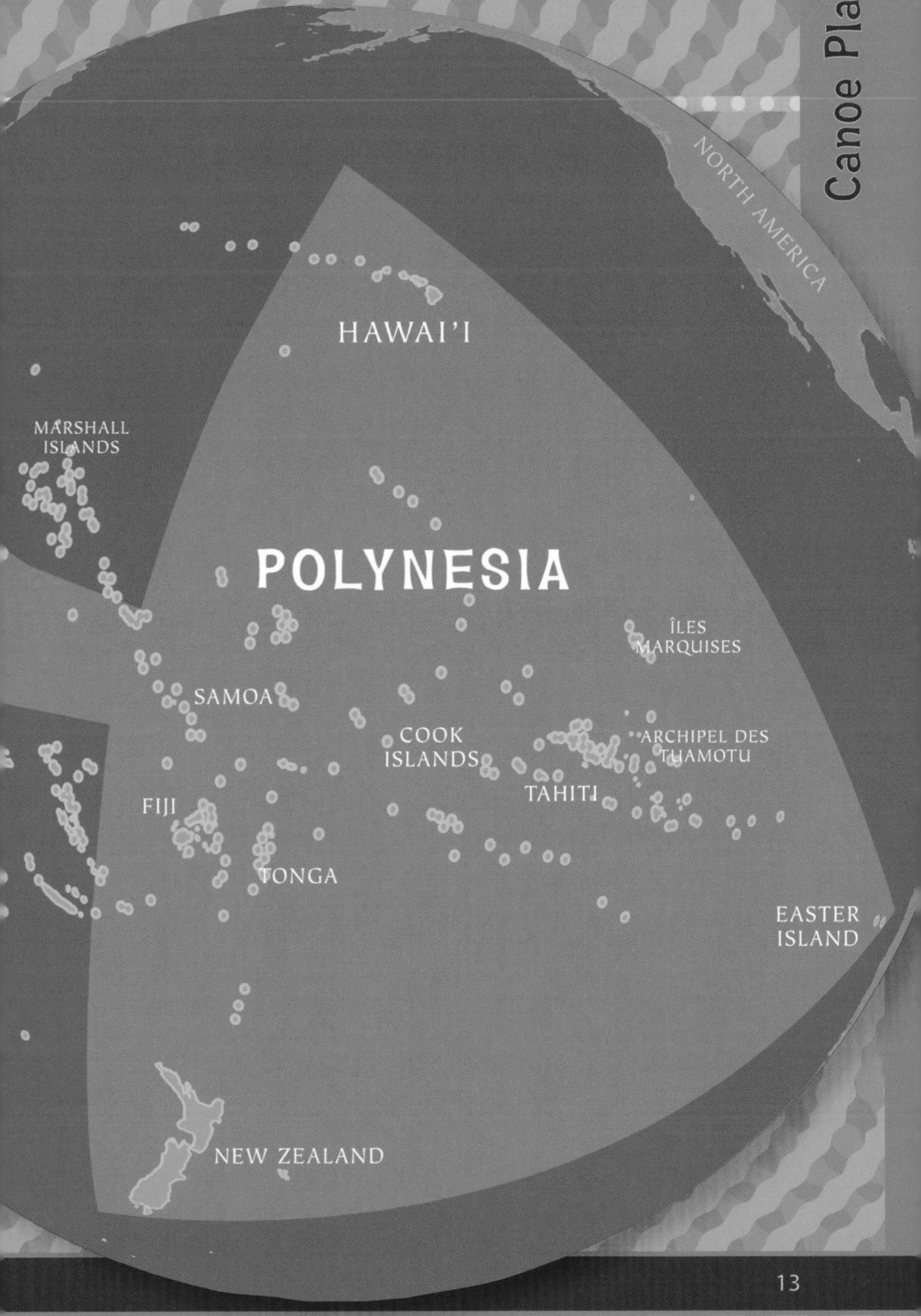

NORTH AMERICA

HAWAI'I

MARSHALL
ISLANDS

POLYNESIA

ÎLES
MARQUISES

SAMOA

COOK
ISLANDS

ARCHIPEL DES
TUAMOTU

TAHITI

FIJI

TONGA

EASTER
ISLAND

NEW ZEALAND

Banana

mai'a (**mah**-*ee-'ah*)

`Musa sp.`

The first Hawaiian people used all parts of the banana plant. Its fruit was good to eat. One enormous leaf could serve as an umbrella and its stalk could act as a roller to help canoeists get their boats into the sea. Children sometimes slid down hills on banana leaf "sleds."

Today, many varieties of bananas are grown in the Hawaiian Islands. You might want to stop by one of the local farmers' markets if you are curious to find out what an apple banana or ice cream banana tastes like.

Breadfruit

ʻulu (ʻoo-loo)

Artocarpus altilis

The breadfruit tree provided early Hawaiian settlers with many useful materials—fruit for nourishment, wood for canoes, and leaves for wrapping food. Breadfruit's sticky sap was used to treat stomachaches and also to caulk canoes!

Did you know?

The texture and taste of a breadfruit is similar to that of a potato. One breadfruit can weigh as much as thirteen pounds. That's heavier than most pet cats!

Candlenut Tree

kukui (koo-**koo**-ee)

Aleurites moluccana

The nuts from this tree provided the first Hawaiians with a source of light. The inner kernels of the nuts were removed and strung on a skewer of bamboo or on the midrib of a coconut frond. The first nut was set on fire. As that nut burned down, the second nut would catch on fire, and so on until all the nuts had been burned. In addition to providing light, kukui nuts were also used to make leis.

Coconut

niu (*nee-oo*)

Cocos nucifera

No wonder early Polynesians brought the coconut palm with them! Nearly every part of this tree can be used in some way. Leaves can be woven into hats, mats, or baskets. Trunks provide housing material. Coconuts contain liquid to drink and meat to eat. Empty shells make handy bowls, and coconut husk can be woven into rope.

Did you know?

Coconuts begin producing fruit in their seventh year and continue producing fruit for approximately seventy years.

Taro

kalo (*kah*-lo)

Colocasia esculenta

Kalo was a staple source of food for the early Hawaiians. Its underground stems could be cooked or pounded into a paste called poi. Kalo's heart-shaped leaves taste a bit like spinach.

Did you know?

The kalo plant is full of a chemical compound called calcium oxalate. This compound forms in sharp crystals. If kalo is eaten raw, then ouch!—the crystals can irritate a person's mouth or throat. Cooking breaks down the calcium oxalate so the plant can be eaten with a smile instead of a grimace.

Paper Mulberry

wauke (***wah***-*oo-keh*)

Broussonetia papyrifera

The inner bark of wauke was beaten to make kapa, a soft, white cloth used for clothing, bedding, and decorations. Polynesians stamped geometric designs on the cloth using bamboo tools. The designs were colored using dyes made from local plants. *Kapa* means "the beaten."

Shampoo Ginger

'awapuhi kuahiwi
(*'ah-wah-**poo**-hee koo-ah-**hee**-wee*)

Zingiber zerumbet

How did Polynesians get shampoo from this plant? The flower heads contain a sudsy liquid that can be used to clean hair. Its fragrant underground stems were often stored with kapa to make the cloth smell good.

Sugar Cane

kō (ko)

Saccharum officinarum

Sugar cane is a large grass. Its stalks travel well and are easily planted. The first Hawaiian settlers used the juice of sugar cane to sweeten food and medicine.

Today, we still use sugar cane as a sweetener. Harvested sugar cane is sent to factories that grind up the stalks to release the cane's juice. The juice is then boiled and allowed to evaporate. Evaporated cane juice is more commonly known as granulated sugar!

Flowers

Anthurium

Anthurium sp.

These waxy, heart-shaped flowers come in a variety of colors and are popular as cut flowers. The plants are native to South America and were introduced to O'ahu over one hundred years ago.

Bird of Paradise

Strelitzia reginae

To some people, the flowers
of this plant look like a bird's
beak with orange tufts of
head feathers. To others, the
flower resembles a colorful
bird in flight. Either way, bird
of paradise is a descriptive
name for this plant, a native
of South Africa.

Bougainvillea

pukanawila (poo-**kah**-nah-vee-lah)

Bougainvillea sp.

Bougainvillea was named after a French admiral, Louis de Bougainville, who saw these vines growing in South America in the 1760s and decided to bring some back to France. Since then, bougainvillea has become a popular tropical plant around the world. Europeans brought it to Hawai'i over 150 years ago.

Did you know?

The flowers of most bougainvilleas are white! The colorful parts of the plants are actually modified leaves called bracts.

Bromeliad

Bromeliaceae sp.

Bromeliads come in many forms and grow in a variety of ways. Pineapples are the only edible member of the bromeliad family.

Did you know?

Many bromeliads are epiphytes (ep·i·fites). Epiphytes are plants that can take in nutrients and moisture from the air around them so they don't need soil in which to grow. Instead of growing in dirt, epiphytes often grow on other plants or rocks.

Heliconia

Heliconia sp.

Many of these plants, native to South America, originally grew in people's gardens here in Hawai'i. Some escaped cultivation, however, and now grow in the wild. Heliconias grow from underground stems and are related to other plants listed in this book—the traveler's palm, banana, bird of paradise, and ginger.

Hibiscus

aloalo (*ah-lo-**ah**-lo*)

Hibiscus sp.

Hibiscus is a native Hawaiian shrub with many variations and hybrids. The yellow hibiscus is Hawai'i's state flower.

Orchid

'okika (*'o-**kee**-kah*)

The orchid family is one of the largest families of flowering plants on earth. Since the list of its botanical names would be longer than this page, just the common English and Hawaiian names are given here.

Most of the orchids you see growing in Hawai'i are native to other countries, but grow very well in the islands' warm, moist air.

Did you know?

The flavor of vanilla comes from the seed pod of a species of vanilla orchid. Vanilla orchids grow as vines and are cultivated on the island of Hawai'i.

Plumeria

pua melia
(**poo**-ah meh-**lee**-ah)

Plumeria sp.

Plumeria's thick, sweet-smelling flowers
are often used for making leis. During the winter,
most plumeria trees drop their leaves, leaving
their branches bare.

Yellow Ginger

'awapuhi melemele
(*'ah-wah-**poo**-hee meh-leh **meh**-leh*)

Hedychium flavescens

This fragrant flower, originally from India, now grows wild in Hawai'i and is also used to make leis.

Silversword

ʻāhinahina
(*ʻah-hee-nah-**hee**-nah*)

Argyroxiphium sandwicense

Native Hawaiian silversword plants can be seen in Haleakala National Park on Maui or on Mauna Kea on the island of Hawaiʻi . Silverswords grow for a long time—as much as forty years—before they flower! As soon as the spectacular flower show is over, the plant dies.

Silversword are an endangered species. They nearly went extinct after humans introduced grazing animals such as cattle and sheep to Hawaiʻi .

Fruits and Nuts

Coffee

kope (**ko**-*peh*)

Coffea arabica

The red, ripe fruit of the
coffee plant usually contains
one or two seeds. These
seeds are known as coffee
beans. In order to produce
coffee, the seeds are separated
from the fruit and dried. The
dried coffee beans are green.
These green beans need to be
roasted and ground before a
cup of coffee can be made.

Chocolate

Theobroma cacao

Did you know?

Theobroma is Greek for "food of the gods." Hawai'i is the only U.S. state that grows cacao commercially.

Chocolate is made from the seeds of cacao (kuh-kow) pods. Once the seeds are harvested, they need to be fermented and dried before they are ready to be made into chocolate. The dried beans are then roasted and ground up into a chocolate paste. Once the paste is made, then ingredients such as sugar can be added to produce the tasty confection we call chocolate.

Guava

kuawa (*koo-**ah**-vah*)

Psidium guajava

Depending on the type of guava grown, the inside of the fruit may be red, yellow, pink, or white. Kuawa are often used to make juice or jelly. If you hike around Hawai'i, look for guava trees growing in the wild. Their colorful bark makes them easy to identify.

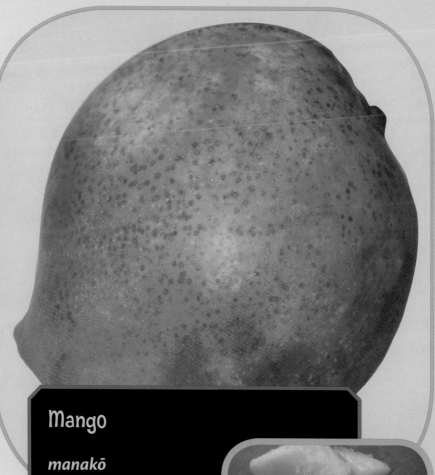

Mango

manakō
*(mah-nah-**ko**)*

Mangifera indica

Mangoes are native to
Southeast Asia and India.
This large-seeded fruit
didn't arrive in Hawaiʻi
until the 1820s. Mangoes
are a popular fruit that
is eaten raw, made into
smoothies, or pickled!

Papaya

mīkana
(mee-**kah**-nah)

Carica papaya

To eat a papaya, many people cut the fruit in half, discard the black seeds, and then scoop out the sweet flesh with a spoon.

Did you know?

Papayas are one of the fastest-growing fruit "trees" in the world. If you planted a papaya seed today, you would be able to harvest ripe fruit in less than two years! Since the papaya plant does not have a woody stem, it's technically not a tree. Instead, it's a giant herb.

Pineapple

hala-kahiki
(**hah**-lah kah-**hee**-kee)

Ananas comosus

Did you know?

Pineapples don't grow on trees. They are the fruit of a bromeliad plant.

Even though the pineapple has become a symbol for Hawai'i, the plant didn't arrive here until Captain James Cook's voyage in the late 1700s. Pineapples are native to South America. There, they are called *ananas*, which means "excellent fruit." When Europeans saw the fruit for the first time, they thought it resembled a pinecone. Its flesh reminded them of apples. So, they gave this fruit the name of pineapple.

Macadamia Nut

Macadamia integrifolia

When these trees arrived from Australia in the 1880s, they were used as an ornamental plant. Hawai'i's macadamia nut production didn't take off until the 1950s. Now, Hawai'i is the world's largest supplier. Shelled macadamia nuts are turned into oil, used in cooking and baking, or eaten by themselves.

Did you know?

Macadamia nuts are famous for being one of the hardest nuts to crack open!

Rambutan

Nephelium lappaceum

These spiky fruits, native to Southeast Asia, turn bright red when they are ripe. To eat a rambutan, cut open the rind and pop out the white edible portion. After you remove the seed inside, you may enjoy the rest of the fruit.

Trees

Banyan Tree

Ficus benghalensis

These enormous trees, originally from India, are easy to spot in the parks around Hawai'i. If you are traveling to Maui, stop by Banyan Tree Park in Lahaina to see one of the world's largest banyan trees. The tree nearly takes up one city block!

Koa

koa (**ko**-*ah*)

Acacia koa

Koa is Hawai'i's largest native forest tree and is one of the dominant trees in the rainforest canopy. Koa have unusual foliage. The leaves of young trees are small and divided into two rows. As the koa matures, its leaves transform into one broad "leaf." Technically, this new foliage is considered a phyllode (fi-lode) which is a modified leaf stem.

Did you know?

Early Hawaiians used koa logs to make canoes, some of which were seventy feet in length.

ʻŌhiʻa

ʻōhiʻa (*ʻo-**hee**-ʻah*)

Metrosideros polymorpha

ʻŌhiʻa is another dominant tree in Hawaiʻi's rainforest canopy. ʻŌhiʻa blossoms, or lehua (leh-hoo-ah), are sources of nectar for many native birds such as the ʻapapane. Lehua are colored bright red or yellow.

Portia Tree

milo (*mee*-loh)

Thespesia populnea

This tree was probably introduced by the early Polynesians, but some scientists think it might be native as well. Its wood was used to make bowls and paddles. Its fruits were used to make a yellowish-green dye.

Milo make excellent shade trees. Today, you can see these trees growing in parks around Hawai'i .

Screwpine

hala (**hah**-*lah*)

Pandanus tectorius

This tree isn't a pine, but its fruits do resemble pinecones. Many people mistakenly think this is a pineapple tree since, from a distance, its fruits look like pineapples. The large fruit is made up of smaller parts called keys. The inner part of the keys is edible but not very tasty. Scientists believe hala is native to Hawai'i. Early Polynesians wove the hala leaves into mats, hats, and thatching for roofs.

Traveler's Palm

Ravenala madagascariensis

Even though this plant might look like a palm, it isn't. It is closely related, however, to another plant in this book. Can you guess which one? Look at the traveler's palm's flowers for a clue. You guessed it! This plant is closely related to the bird of paradise.

Did you know?

This plant got its name because thirsty travelers could always find water pooled at the base of the stems.

Animals

When the first Polynesians arrived on the Hawaiian Islands nearly two thousand years ago, what kind of animals do you suppose they saw roaming on the land?

Scientists believe the answer is . . .

None!

Birds and fish were plentiful, since they could get to the islands by flying or swimming. A species of bat lived here, too. However, land animals didn't begin living in Hawai'i until the Polynesians arrived with pigs, dogs, and chickens. Rats, geckoes, and skinks showed up on the islands at the same time, too.

Hawaiian monk seal. U.S. Fish and Wildlife Service

These three animals were often stowaways inside the Polynesian canoes.

Ever since then, many other animals have appeared in the Hawaiian Islands in much the same way. They were brought here by humans, either on purpose or by accident. Unfortunately, many introduced species, such as the mongoose, have become pests or hazards to native animals. Since earlier Hawaiian animals evolved without land mammals, they didn't develop a way to protect themselves against teeth and claws.

Birds

'Apapane

'apapane (*'ah-pah-**pah**-neh*)

Himatione sanguinea

Luckily for birdwatchers, 'apapane is one of the more frequently seen native birds in Hawaiian forests. Look for them feeding on nectar from the fuzzy red or yellow blossoms of the 'ōhi'a.

Black-crowned Night Heron

'auku'u (*'ah-oo-koo-'oo*)

Nycticorax nycticorax

'Auku'u can often be spotted trying to catch fish or frogs near watery places such as wetlands and streams. The best time to see them is at dawn or dusk when they are most active. 'Auku'u are the most common kind of heron in the world and are year-round residents of Hawai'i .

Did you know?

Question: In what way are young 'auku'u helpful to scientists who study the diets of birds?

Answer: Young 'auku'u often vomit when they are flustered, so it's easy for scientists to see what these birds have recently eaten!

Cattle Egret

Bubulcus ibis

Cattle egret, originally from Africa, were
introduced to Hawaiʻi approximately fifty years
ago. These birds eat insects so it's not unusual to
see them flying behind lawn mowers, catching
the bugs disturbed by the mowing.

Common Moorhen

ʻalae ʻula
(ʻah-**lah**-eh ʻ**oo**-lah)

Gallinula chloropus sadvicensis

These freshwater birds eat algae, water plants, and insects. Their chicks are able to swim and run soon after they hatch.

Did you know?

According to Hawaiian mythology, ʻalae ʻula once had a white patch on its forehead. When this bird brought fire from the volcano to humans, its white patch turned red from the volcano's flame.

Common Myna

piha ʻekelo
(**pee**-hah ʻeh-**keh**-lo)

Acridotheres tristis

Mynas are very adaptable birds. They eat everything from insects to leftover human food. Mynas were introduced to Hawaiʻi from India over a hundred years ago. Now, they are one of the most commonly seen birds on the islands. Mynas are easy to identify by their bright yellow beak, feet, and eye patch.

Did you know?

Mynas are a popular pet because of their ability to mimic many sounds. Some pet mynas have been able to imitate over one hundred human words! No wonder this bird's Hawaiian name means full of voice.

Hawaiian Coot

'alae kea (*'al-**lah**-ee **keh**-ah*)

Fulcia alai

Coots live in wetland habitats. Their lobed feet help them to paddle in water and to walk across mud or even floating plants! 'Alae kea eat plants, small fish, and insects.

Hawaiian Goose

*nēnē (**neh**-neh)*

Branta sandvicensis

The endangered nēnē is native to Hawaiʻi and is the state's bird. Since nēnē often live near lava flows instead of water, their feet are more padded and less webbed than those of other species of geese. This feature allows nēnē to walk across lava flows more easily.

Java Sparrow

Padda oryzivora

Java sparrows have been in Hawai'i since the 1860s. Look for these small birds hunting for seeds in grassy parks such as Kapiolani Park on O'ahu.

Did you know?

Java sparrows are sometimes called Java rice birds. In their native land of Indonesia, they are considered pests since they like to eat rice plants. In some parts of the U.S. mainland, Java sparrows are banned as pets because of the fear that if they get loose, they will damage agricultural crops there as well.

Did you know?

Squid is one of the albatross's main sources of food. Since squid often rise to the surface of the sea at night, the Laysan albatross have developed especially keen night vision in order to see their prey.

Laysan Albatross

moli (**moh**-*lee*)

Phoebastria immutabilis

Laysan albatross are sometimes called a "goony bird" because they are not very graceful walking on land. These birds spend half of the year at sea and often don't touch ground until mating season. Moli often return each year to the same nesting site. In a residential neighborhood in Princeville, Kaua'i, homeowners have had the same albatross couple return to their yard every fall for years to build a nest and rear their babies!

Pacific Golden Plover

kōlea (*ko-leh-ah*)

Pluvialis fulva

These native Hawaiian birds spend their summers nesting in Alaska. In early fall, kōlea head back home by flying nonstop for two days! Pacific golden plovers are one of the few native birds that are easily seen in Hawai'i. Look for them in grassy parks or along the shore.

Red-crested Cardinal

Paroaria coronata

This cardinal's pointy, red head and white underside make it easy to recognize. Like most cardinals, the red-crested has a thick, cone-shaped beak—perfect for cracking open hard seeds. This species is native to South America and is sometimes called the Brazilian cardinal. Red-crested cardinals have lived in Hawai'i since 1930 and are frequently seen in urban parks.

Did you know?

These birds got the nickname of "tattler" because they often give alarm calls when they sense danger is nearby.

Wandering Tattler

ʻūlili (ʻoo-**lee**-lee)

Heteroscelus incanus

Tattlers are winter visitors to Hawaiʻi. They can often be seen wandering around shorelines by themselves. Tattlers poke their long bills into sand or under rocks to find shellfish or insects.

White-rumped Shama

Copsychus malabaricus

White-rumped shamas, originally from southern Asia, were often kept as pets because of their beautiful singing ability. In fact, the song of the white-rumped shama was one of the first birdsongs ever recorded! These birds were introduced to Hawaiʻi in 1940 and like to make their homes in forests.

Zebra Dove

Geopelia striata

Zebra doves are frequently seen pecking for seeds on the ground and in the grass. Even though they are a common bird, they have an uncommon ability. Most bird parents need to hunt for food to feed to their babies. But not dove parents! Both male and female doves are able to produce a substance called crop milk to feed their babies. Chicks are able to drink this milk by poking their beaks into their parents' open mouths.

Did you know?

A bird's crop is like an empty sac, located near the bottom of its esophagus. When doves become parents, their crops produce a thick, white substance called crop milk.

Insects
and Bugs

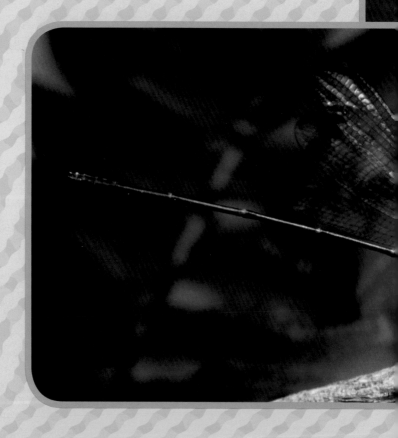

Did you know?

The Kamehameha butterfly is named in honor of Hawaiʻi's King Kamehameha I.

Kamehameha Butterfly

pulelehua *(poo-leh-leh-**hoo**-ah)*

Vanessa tameamea

Hawaiʻi has only two native butterflies and the Kamehameha is one of them. (The other is called the koa butterfly.) The caterpillar of the pulelehua feeds on the leaves of māmaki, a Hawaiian nettle.

Monarch Butterfly

lepelepe-o-Hina (leh-**peh**-leh-peh-o-**hee**-nah)

Danaus plexippus

Monarchs have lived in Hawai'i for over 150 years. The main source of food for monarch caterpillars is the milkweed plant. These plants contain a poison that caterpillars can eat without harm. After the caterpillar turns into a monarch, the poison still remains in its body, causing it to taste horrible to predators.

If you are on the island of O'ahu or Hawai'i, keep your eyes out for an unusual form of the lepelepe-o-Hina fluttering around—a white monarch!

American Cockroach

'elelū (*'eh-leh-**loo***)

Periplaneta americana

Hawai'i has many species of cockroaches. The American cockroach is one of the biggest. It can reach a size of one meter (39.3 inches) in Hawai'i. Just kidding! They only seem that big. Adult American cockroaches are actually about four centimeters (1.6 inches) and are often nicknamed "747s" or "B2 Bombers" after large airplanes.

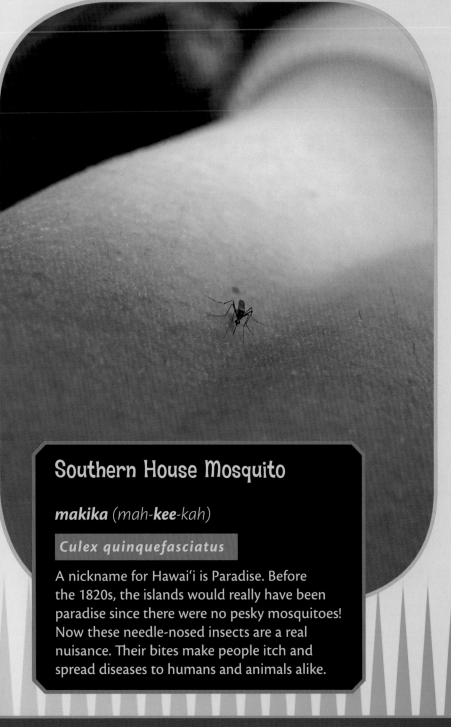

Southern House Mosquito

makika (mah-**kee**-kah)

Culex quinquefasciatus

A nickname for Hawai'i is Paradise. Before the 1820s, the islands would really have been paradise since there were no pesky mosquitoes! Now these needle-nosed insects are a real nuisance. Their bites make people itch and spread diseases to humans and animals alike.

Land Reptiles
and Mammals

Green Anole

Anolis carolinensis

Green anoles are not always green. They are able to change color from bright green to brown or gray depending on their environment. Male anoles have a flap of skin under their neck called a dewlap. Dewlaps inflate to attract mates or to act as territorial displays. Green anoles, native to the Southeastern United States, were introduced to Hawai'i over fifty years ago. They eat insects and spiders.

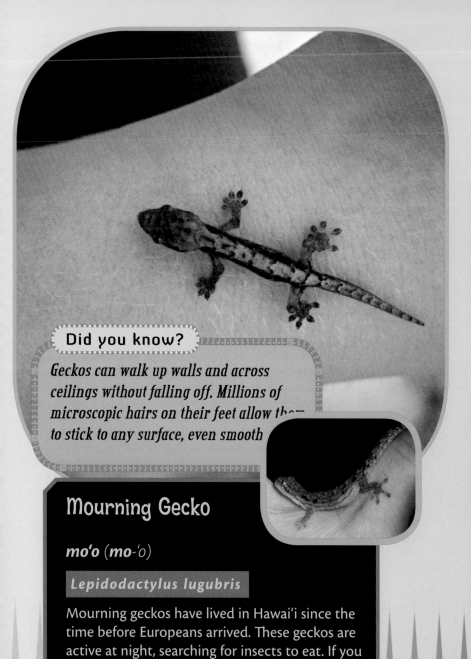

Did you know?

Geckos can walk up walls and across ceilings without falling off. Millions of microscopic hairs on their feet allow them to stick to any surface, even smooth

Mourning Gecko

mo'o (mo-'o)

Lepidodactylus lugubris

Mourning geckos have lived in Hawai'i since the time before Europeans arrived. These geckos are active at night, searching for insects to eat. If you hear a chirping or clicking noise coming from a gecko, don't be surprised. Geckos are one of the few lizards capable of making sounds.

Mongoose

manakuke *(mah-nah-**koo**-keh)*

Herpestes javanicus

Manakuke were introduced to Hawai'i in the late 1800s to help control the rat problem on sugar cane plantations. Unfortunately, instead of eating rats, the mongooses preferred to eat native birds and their eggs. Since manakuke don't have natural predators in Hawai'i, their population has increased. As a result, Hawai'i's native bird population has decreased.

Pig

pua'a (*poo-**ah**-'ah*)

Sus scrofa

Hawai'i's wild pigs are a nuisance. They root up native plants and cause the soil to erode. Large, European pigs were introduced to Hawai'i with the arrival of Captain James Cook. The Polynesian pigs were much smaller. Scientists aren't sure if today's wild pigs are a direct descent of the European pigs or if they're a cross between the little and big pigs.

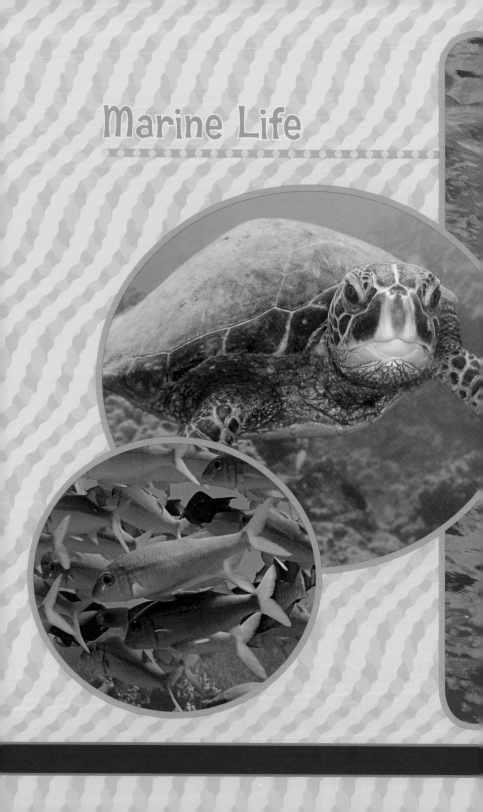

Marine Life

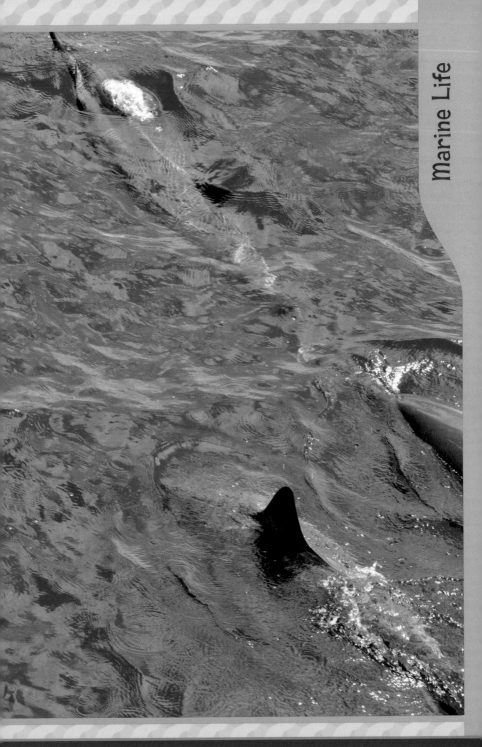

Blueline Surgeonfish

maiko (**mah**-*ee-ko*)

Acanthurus nigroris Valenciennes

To better camouflage itself, this surgeonfish can quickly change to a dark color with a white band around its tail.

Did you know?

Hawai'i has over twenty species of surgeonfish (also called tangs). These fish got their name from the knife-sharp spines at the base of their tail fins. The spines can cut into other fish much like a doctor's scalpel can cut into people. Surgeonfish are one of the most common reef fish seen in Hawai'i. Unicornfish are also a part of the surgeonfish family.

Convict Tang

manini (mah-**nee**-nee)

Acanthurus triostegus

In Hawai'i, the manini is the most abundant member of the surgeonfish family. Its stripes resemble the stripes that convicts used to wear on their jail uniforms

Orangespine Unicornfish

umaumalei (*oo-mah-oo-mah-leh-ee*)

Naso lituratus

This fish's Hawaiian name means "chest garland." The line that runs from its eye to its mouth makes this fish look like it's wearing some kind of lei! Orangespine unicornfish are also called the lipstick tang because of their bright orange lips.

Ringtail Surgeonfish

pualu (*poo-**ah**-loo*)

Acanthurus blochii Valenciennes

The white band around its tail and yellow patch
behind its eye makes this surgeonfish stand out
from the more common varieties.

Bluestripe Snapper

Lutjanus kasmira

These bright yellow fish with four blue stripes like to swim in schools. Bluestripe snappers are one of the few reef fish that aren't native to Hawai'i. They were introduced here in the late 1950s as a potential source of food.

Hawaiian Whitespotted Toby

Canthigaster jactator

This green-eyed fish is the most common species of toby in Hawai'i. Its scientific name, *jactator*, means "bragger." What do you suppose tobies brag about? Maybe the fact that they can puff up their bodies when frightened?

Lagoon Triggerfish

humuhumunukunukua-pua'a
(hoo-moo-hoo-moo-noo-koo-noo-koo-ah-
poo-ah-'ah) or *humuhumu* for short

Rhinecanthus aculeatus

The lagoon triggerfish and its close
relative, the reef triggerfish, are both called
Humuhumunukunukuapua'a in Hawaiian. The
name means "snout like a pig." The humuhumu
is Hawai'i's state fish.

Parrotfish

uhu (oo-hoo)

Scarus sp.

Did you know?

One parrotfish can process up to one ton of sand a year?

The next time you walk on sand in Hawai'i, think about the parrotfish. Why? Because parrotfish eat algae that live in coral. To get to the algae, parrotfish use their fused teeth to bite the coral. Since the fish can't digest this material, all that ground-up coral exits the fish's back end as sand!

Snowflake Moray Eel

puhi kāpā (poo-*hee *kah-*pah)

Echidna nebulosa

Did you know?

Moray eels are members of the fish family.

If you see a moray opening and closing its mouth over and over again, don't worry. That's just the way morays breathe. That motion doesn't mean the eel feels frightened or is ready to attack. While many moray eels have sharp teeth, snowflake eels do not. They use their blunt teeth to crush prey such as crabs.

Blue Rice Coral

ko'a (**ko-***'ah*)

Montipora flabellate

Rice coral comes in a variety of forms and colors depending on its reef environment. It gets its name from the tiny projections that resemble grains of rice.

Did you know?

Ko'a means any type of coral in Hawai'i.

Did you know?

*Coral skeletons are white. The color of most coral comes from an algae called zooxanthellae (zo-**zan**-thel-ee) living inside the polyp.*

Cauliflower Coral

*ko'a (**ko**-'ah)*

Pocillopora meandrina

Even though coral looks like it may be rock, it's not. Coral is made of colonies of tiny animals called coral polyps. Polyps use calcite, a mineral found in seawater, to make hard skeletons for themselves. Cauliflower coral is one of the most common corals in Hawai'i. It comes in a range of colors—from browns to pinks.

Did you know?

The slate pencil urchin got its name because its thick spines were once used to write on chalkboards!

Slate Pencil Urchin

hā'uke'uke 'ula 'ula
(hah-'oo-keh-**'oo**-keh 'oo-lah-**'oo**-lah)

Heterocentrotus mammillatus

Sea urchins have round or oval bodies covered in spines. These spines help protect the animal from predators. Urchins also use their spines, aided by their tube feet, to help them move. A sea urchin's mouth is located on its underside. Sea urchins eat algae and seaweed.

Green Sea Turtle

honu (***hoh***-*noo*)

Chelonia mydas

Honu are one of the largest species of sea turtles. Adults can weigh over four hundred pounds! Honu begin their lives as carnivores that eat crabs and jellyfish. Adults, however, are herbivores that eat algae and sea grass. The algae contribute to the green color of this sea turtle's meat and fat!

Due to habitat destruction and overhunting, honu are listed as an endangered species. Please keep a respectful distance from these turtles if you see one on a beach or while snorkeling.

Hawaiian Monk Seal

'īlioholoikauaua
('ee-lee-oh-hoh-loh-ee-ka-
oo-**ah**-oo-ah)

Monachus schauinslandi

Monk seals, an endangered species, are native to the Hawaiian Islands. Their Hawaiian name means "dog that runs in rough water." Monk seals spend most of their time in the ocean foraging for food such as fish and eels. Sometimes, though, they like to rest on beaches. If you see one resting, please be respectful. Look for as long as you want, but don't approach or disturb the seal.

Did you know?

Monk seals replace their coats once a year through a process called molting. When the seals shed their old skin and hair, a new coat is ready to go!

Humpback Whale

koholā (koh-hoh-**lah**)

Monachus schauinslandi

Humpback whale skull

Humpbacks spend the spring and summer months in Alaska feeding on small fish and krill. In fall, they migrate to Hawai'i to give birth and nurse their young. When koholā babies are born, they are as long as a truck and weigh over a ton. In adulthood, humpbacks are as long as three trucks and weigh over forty tons!

Did you know?

Maui is one of the best islands from which to see humpbacks from December to April.

Spinner Dolphin

nai'a (**nah**-*ee-'ah*)

Stenella longirostris

Spinner dolphins are named for the way they leap out of the ocean and spin several times before they dive back into the sea.

Did you know?

Nai'a don't breathe unconsciously like humans do. Spinner dolphins have to think before breathing. In order to get the rest they need, nai'a sleep with half of their brains awake and half of their brains asleep!

Index

Photo and Illustration Credits and Sources

Pages i: Beach scene on the island of Oahu, Hawaii. Photo credit: Carol M. Highsmith's America, Library of Congress, Prints and Photographs Division. (http://www.loc.gov/pictures/item/2010630473)

Page ii: Lesser frigatebird perching on branch, Midway Atoll National Wildlife Refuge. Photo credit: Michael Lusk, U.S. Fish and Wildlife Service. (http://www.fws.gov/midway); Green sea turtle (Chelonia mydas), Midway Atoll National Wildlife Refuge. Photo credit: Michael Lusk, U.S. Fish and Wildlife Service. (http://www.fws.gov/digitalmedia/cdm4/item_viewer.php?CISOROOT=/natdiglib&CISOPTR=6630&CISOBOX=1&REC=1)

Pages ii–iii (background image), Punalu'u Black Sand Beach on the Big Island, Hawaii. Photo credit: Carol M. Highsmith's America, Library of Congress, Prints and Photographs Division. (http://www.loc.gov/pictures/item/2010630043/)

Pages iv–v: Waterfall in the mountains of Hawaii. Photo credit: Carol M. Highsmith's America, Library of Congress, Prints and Photographs Division. (http://www.loc.gov/pictures/item/2010630466/)

Page vi: Hakalau Forest National Wildlife Refuge, Hawaii. Photo credit: Jim Clark, U.S. Fish and Wildlife Service. (http://www.fws.gov/digitalmedia/cdm4/item_viewer.php?CISOROOT=/natdiglib&CISOPTR=529)

Page vii: NASA, Visible Earth project: Hawaii. Credit: Jacques Descloitres, MODIS Rapid Response Team, NASA/GSFC.

Pages viii–1: USGS Hawaiian Volcano Observatory, Hawaii Volcanoes National Park. Photo credit: Michael Poland , U.S. Geological Survey. (http://gallery.usgs.gov/photos/08_18_2010_h41Ogs6FEa_08_18_2010_17)

Page 1: USGS: Pu`u `O`o Lava fountain. Photo credit: C. Heliker. (http://hvo.wr.usgs.gov/gallery/kilauea/erupt/19930221_caption.html). For more see, the Selected Images of the Pu'u 'O'o-Kupaianaha Eruption, 1983–1997 Album at http://pubs.usgs.gov/dds/dds-80/album.html.

Page 3: Volcano Illustration: RD Studio.

Page 5: http://gallery.usgs.gov/photos/?p=06_21_2010_h40Nfr5EEy_06_21_2010_9

Page 5: Lava flow. A small open channel of lava was entering the water at one of two entry points at the west Waikupanaha entry area, Kilauea, Hawaii, Nov 15 2009. Photo credit: U.S. Geological Survey. (http://gallery.usgs.gov/photos/?p=06_21_2010_h40Nfr5EEy_06_21_2010_9)

Page 7: Diamond Head, side view. Photo credit: Mar1865. (http://en.wikipedia.org/wiki/File:Diamond_Head_Hawaii_From_Round_Top_Rd.JPG#file). Top photo: Hanauma Bay, Oahu, Hawaii. NASA image by Robert Simmon. (http://earthobservatory.nasa.gov/IOTD/view.php?id=4902)

Pages 10–11: Hakalau Forest National Wildlife Refuge, Hawaii. Photo credit: Jim

dot
dot
books

dotdotbooks.com